BREATHE IT IN!

The Chemistry of **Air**

Written by William D. Adams

WORLD BOOK

www.worldbook.com

Co-published by agreement between Shi Tu Hui and World Book, Inc.

Shi Tu Hui
Room 1807, Block 1,
#3 West Dawang Road
Chaoyang District, Beijing 100025
P.R. China

World Book, Inc.
180 North LaSalle Street
Suite 900
Chicago, Illinois 60601
USA

© 2026. All rights reserved. This volume may not be reproduced in whole or in part in any form without prior written permission from the publisher.

WORLD BOOK and the GLOBE DEVICE are registered trademarks or trademarks of World Book, Inc.

Library of Congress Control Number: 2025942237

Aha! Academy: Chemistry
ISBN: 978-0-7166-7346-0 (set, hardcover)

Breathe It In! The Chemistry of Air
ISBN: 978-0-7166-7350-7 (hard cover)
ISBN: 978-0-7166-7370-5 (e-book)
ISBN: 978-0-7166-7360-6 (soft cover)

Staff

Editorial

Vice President
Tom Evans

Senior Manager, New Content
Jeff De La Rosa

Senior Curriculum Designer
Caroline Davidson

Curriculum Designer
Mikayla Kightlinger

Content Creator
Joseph P. Cataliotti

Proofreader
Nathalie Strassheim

Indexer
Nathaniel Lindstrom

Graphics and Design

Senior Visual
Communications Designer
Melanie Bender

Designer
Shannon Hagman

Written by William D. Adams

Designed by Starletta Polster

Acknowledgments

The publishers gratefully acknowledge the following sources for photography. All illustrations were prepared by WORLD BOOK unless otherwise noted.

Cover: 220 Selfmade studio/Shutterstock; Elisa Manzati/Shutterstock; Ian Dewar Photography/Shutterstock; IrinaK/Shutterstock; lev radin/Shutterstock

© The Print Collector/Alamy 17, 46; © SO-Photography/Alamy 41; © Sueddeutsche Zeitung Photo/Alamy 15; © Envionrmental XPRT/The CMM Group 38, 39; © Central Press/Stringer/Getty Images 31; Global Monitoring Laboratory/NOAA 21; Public Domain (Science History Institute) 17; © Shutterstock 3, 4, 5, 6, 7, 8, 9, 10, 11, 12, 13, 14, 15, 16, 17, 18, 19, 20, 21, 22, 23, 24, 25, 26, 27, 28, 29, 30, 31, 32, 33, 34, 35, 36, 37, 38, 39, 40, 41, 42, 43, 44, 45, 46, 47, 48

There is a glossary of terms on page 48. Terms defined in the glossary are in type that looks like *this* on their first appearance on any spread (two facing pages).

Contents

Introduction 4

① **The atmosphere** 6
    Reactions in the atmosphere 8
    Vital molecule: ozone 10

② **Air as a resource** 12
    Vital element: nitrogen 14
    Combustion 16

③ **Global warming** 18
    Vital molecule: carbon dioxide 20
    Greenhouse effect 22
    Other greenhouse gases 24

④ **Air pollution** 26
    The stench of combustion 28
    Smog out 30
    Other sources of air pollution 32
    Air pollution and the environment 34

⑤ **Cleaning up the air** 36
    Controlling pollution 38
    Fighting global warming 40
    What can YOU do? 42

Experimenting with air 44
Index 46
Glossary 48

Introduction

Air is all around you. You need it to live. But because you can't see it, it's easy to forget about it. Just like everything else, air is made up of *molecules,* which are in turn made of *atoms*.

Are those molecules just hanging there, idly suspended near Earth's surface? No! The molecules that make up air are bouncing around at hundreds of miles or kilometers per hour and undergoing *chemical reactions* with one another, the ground, water, and living things.

Humans have learned how to put the molecules in the air to work for us. We've also used the air as a dumping ground for pollution, the byproducts of chemical reactions. The unintended consequences of these uses will affect us for generations. But, we can take steps to counteract these changes in the air. Read on to find out more about the chemistry of air!

1
THE ATMOSPHERE

An atmosphere is the mass of gases that surrounds a planet or other heavenly body. Earth's atmosphere is a big part of what makes this planet so great for living things! It distributes heat around the surface, keeps water from escaping into space, and blocks harmful rays from the sun. Naturally, it's also taken in by living things in the processes of respiration and photosynthesis.

What is both invisible and blue, both a radiator and a blanket, feels weightless but is immensely heavy, and is necessary for life? The answer is: Earth's *atmosphere!*

But, the atmosphere isn't an idle mass of gas! Just like everything in the universe, the air is made of atoms and *molecules*. These molecules can break apart and recombine to form new molecules. They can react with one another, or they can react with other molecules at Earth's surface.

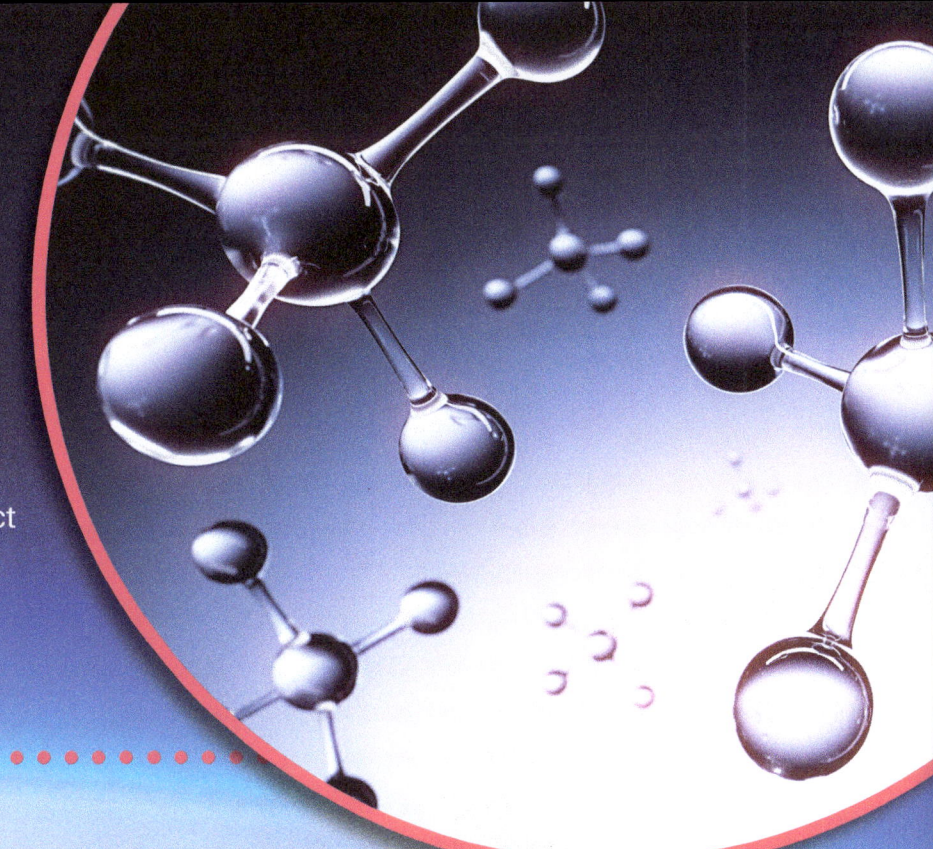

I've got a Titan-ic atmosphere!

DID YOU KNOW?

The weight of Earth's atmosphere is about 5.5 quadrillion tons! Other rocky planets and moons have atmospheres, too, from the thin, wispy atmosphere of Mars to the soupy clouds of Saturn's moon Titan.

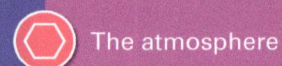
The atmosphere

Reactions in the atmosphere

Light from the sun can change the molecules found in the *atmosphere*. *Photochemistry* is the branch of chemistry that deals with the **chemical reactions** that result when the molecules of a substance absorb light. Light is absorbed in tiny packets of energy called photons. When a *molecule* absorbs a *photon*, it increases in energy, entering an excited state. In some cases, the molecule gains enough energy to undergo unusual chemical reactions while in the excited state. Such photochemical reactions occur when the molecule absorbs visible or ultraviolet light, which has a short wavelength.

Clean air is totally radical!

The atmosphere cleans itself—to an extent—with photochemistry. A *radical* is a group of two or more charged or neutral atoms that have at least one unpaired electron. Hydroxyl radicals are created from a reaction of water and a molecule called ozone with energy from sunlight. These radicals can break down some pollutants, such as climate-altering methane gas.

The atmosphere is a veritable chemistry lab! Its molecules undergo constant *chemical reactions*.

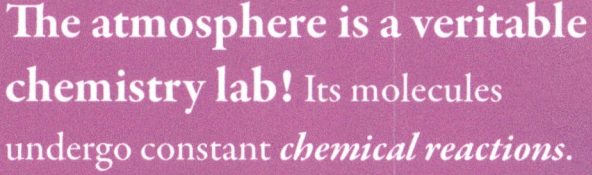

Lightning has a shocking secret—it causes several chemical reactions in the atmosphere. When lightning strikes, the intense heat and electrical energy cause some of the nitrogen and oxygen in the air to combine, forming nitrogen oxides. These nitrogen oxides then dissolve in rainwater, creating nitrates that can act as natural fertilizers in the soil. Additionally, the high temperatures of lightning can split water molecules in the air, producing hydrogen and oxygen gases.

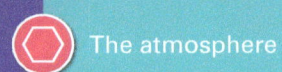

The atmosphere

Vital molecule: ozone

STATS

Chemical formula

O_3

Lifetime in atmosphere: From 1 week to 1 month

Appearance Colorless or pale blue gas

High up in the atmosphere, ozone blocks harmful ultraviolet rays from the sun. Such rays can damage tissue and cause cancers. It's kind of like planetwide sunblock!

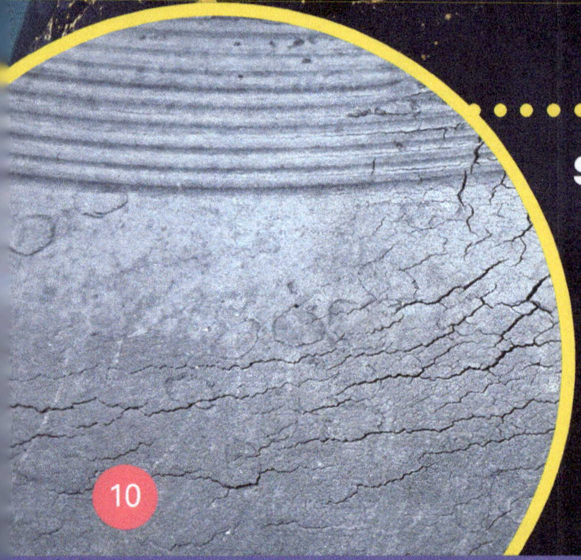

Sometimes the location makes the pollutant. Nearer to the ground, ozone is a pollutant. It can harm plant and animal tissues and damage rubber and plastic.

Ozone is a Jekyll-and-Hyde *molecule*. While harmful at ground level, high in the *atmosphere* it protects us from the sun's most damaging rays.

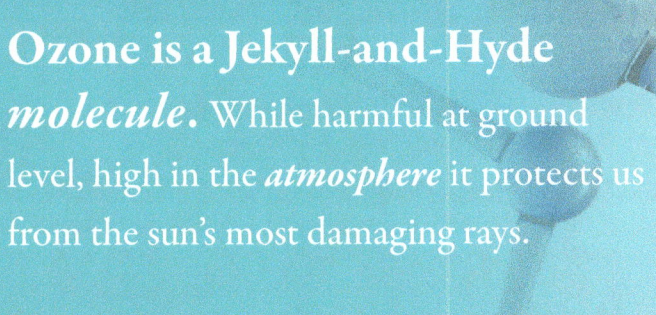

Ozone in the upper atmosphere forms through *photochemical reactions*. Ultraviolet rays from the sun strike oxygen molecules, breaking them into oxygen atoms that then combine with other oxygen molecules to form ozone.

Protecting the **ozone layer** is one of humanity's greatest environmental success stories. In the 1970's, a hole in the ozone layer began appearing each winter over Antarctica. Scientists quickly determined that human-made chemicals called chlorofluorocarbons (CFC's) were causing this hole. CFC's were used for refrigeration and air conditioning. But when CFC's leaked out and reached the upper atmosphere, they broke down into long-lived chemicals that destroyed ozone. The United Nations established the Montreal Protocol in 1987 to quickly phase out the production and use of CFC's. Every country in the world signed the protocol by 2009. Now, the seasonal hole in the ozone layer continues to shrink. Experts think the ozone layer will be completely healed by about 2065. Phew!

2 AIR AS A RESOURCE

You might not think of air as a valuable resource—unless you're an astronaut or a diver! Sure, many living things need air to breathe. But even if we didn't, our lives would be drastically different without air. That's because air is a vital feedstock for the *chemical reactions* that power our lives!

Air is a valuable natural resource! People use the oxygen, nitrogen, and other *molecules* in the air for all kinds of purposes.

DID YOU KNOW?

Earth's *atmosphere* is composed primarily of nitrogen (78%), oxygen (21%), and argon (1%), with small amounts of other gases, such as carbon dioxide and water vapor.

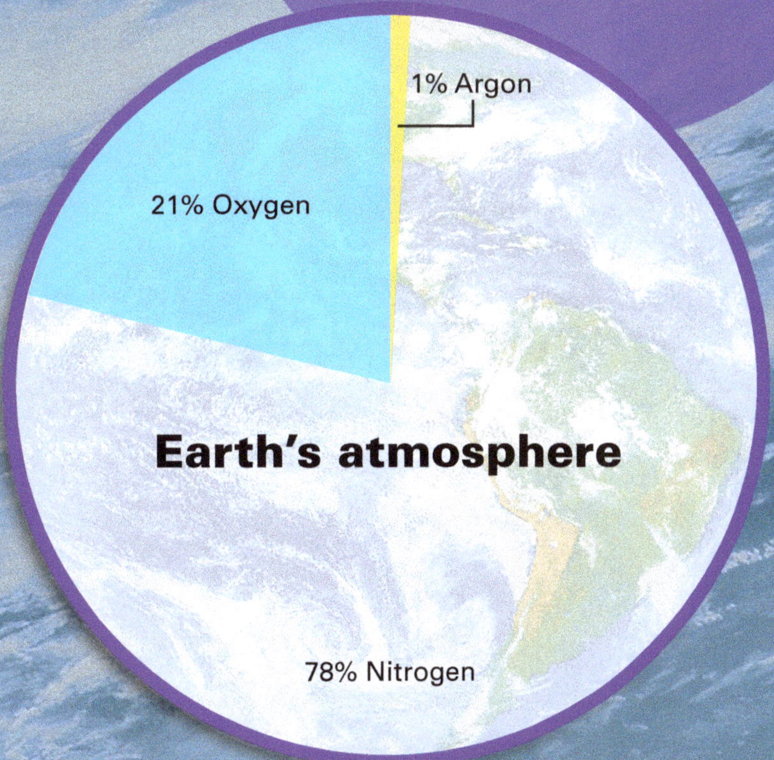

1% Argon

21% Oxygen

Earth's atmosphere

78% Nitrogen

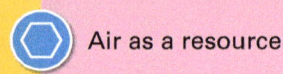 Air as a resource

Vital element: nitrogen

STATS

Symbol
N

Atomic Number
7

Atomic Mass
14.0067

Discoverer
Daniel Rutherford

Nitrogen
$N_2 : N \equiv N$

In the *atmosphere*, elemental nitrogen is found in *molecules* of two atoms joined together by a triple bond (N_2). That means the two atoms share three pairs of electrons. This triple bond makes N_2 molecules extremely hard to break apart.

Carbon, hydrogen, oxygen, and nitrogen are the four most important elements to living things. The first three can be obtained through carbon dioxide, water, and oxygen gas. But because gaseous nitrogen's triple bond is so hard to break, it's not useful to most living things. Only certain bacteria can break the bond to incorporate the nitrogen atoms into organic molecules.

Nitrogen is the most common element in the *atmosphere*. But no animals and very few plants can use atmospheric nitrogen!

Guano for sale!

In the late 1800's, humanity was running into a problem. We needed to grow more food for the exploding population. But, the only source for nitrogen fertilizer was **guano**— bird poop. Gross! German chemist **Fritz Haber** developed a process to break the triple bonds of nitrogen in the air to make fertilizer—no bird poop required! Haber was hailed as a hero for saving humankind from starvation, but his legacy is complicated. A passionate nationalist, he used the process to create gunpowder and even developed chemical weapons for use in World War I (1914-1918).

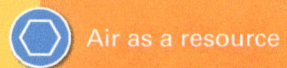 Air as a resource

Combustion

Combustion is a *chemical reaction* that gives off heat and light. It involves the rapid combination of oxygen with a fuel to produce burning. The fuel may be a solid, liquid, or gas. Combustion occurs, for example, when oxygen in the air reacts with charcoal in a barbecue grill. In most cases, combustion occurs between a gaseous fuel and the oxygen in the air. The fuel can start out as a solid or liquid, but it must be *vaporized* (changed to a gas) before it can burn.

The light and heat generated by combustion are incredibly useful. In the past, people used torches, lamps, and candles to light indoor spaces. Combustion is used to run generators in coal and gas power plants. It's also used to power cars and industrial machinery.

Oxygen is like a fuel. Yes, it's a fuel for our bodies and those of many other living things. But, it also readily reacts to form other compounds. One important way it does this is through *combustion.*

When something combusts, it doesn't just disappear! Most combustion involves fuel containing carbon. Such reactions produce carbon dioxide and water vapor.

In the 1700's, scientists were fascinated by burning and what enabled things to burn. They thought that objects that burned gave off a substance called *phlogiston,* which fresh air absorbed. In the late 1700's, French scientist **Antoine Lavoisier** discovered that it was in fact the other way around, with oxygen in the air being absorbed during combustion.

3 GLOBAL WARMING

What's the big deal about a few degrees?

The excess heat is causing heat waves, droughts, and floods to become more frequent and extreme and to last longer. Also, warmer water takes up slightly more space than colder water. This effect stacks up when entire oceans are involved. The result is rising sea levels, causing dangerous flooding.

We live in a warming world. Average temperatures are increasing year on year. This process is called *global warming*. Scientists agree that changes made to the air by human activities are driving the warming pattern.

Global warming is also affecting plant and animal life. *Every species* (kind) has *evolved* (developed over time) to be adapted to particular weather conditions and temperatures. Global warming is causing many species to decline and *go extinct* (die out).

The *atmosphere* is so big. How are people able to affect it? Read on to find out!

Global warming

Vital molecule: carbon dioxide

STATS

Chemical formula

CO_2

Atomic Number
**-109.3 °F
(-78.5 °C)**

Atomic Mass
238.02891

Discoverer
Joseph Black

Carbon dioxide *sublimates* at atmospheric pressure. This means that it goes straight from solid to gaseous form. Solid carbon dioxide is called *dry ice*. People use dry ice to transport things that need to stay cold, but not wet.

Plants use carbon dioxide and water to grow their tissues with the help of sunlight. This process is called *photosynthesis*. Animals generally eat plants or eat animals that eat plants. So in a way, you're made of carbon dioxide. Chew on *that!*

Carbon dioxide is a vital nutrient to plants, a waste gas to animals, and a thermal blanket to Earth. Carbon dioxide's low abundance in the *atmosphere* belies its importance.

Carbon dioxide makes up just 0.04% of Earth's atmosphere! That makes it easier for human actions to make significant changes to its concentration than to those of nitrogen or oxygen.

Most common forms of *combustion* involve fuel containing the element carbon, such as coal, gasoline, wood, and the like. Such fuels combust with oxygen to produce water vapor and carbon dioxide.

$$2C + 2O_2 \rightarrow 2CO_2$$

In 1958, scientists led by Charles Keeling at the Mauna Loa Observatory in Hawaii began tracking levels of carbon dioxide in Earth's atmosphere. These scientists noticed that carbon dioxide levels in the atmosphere were steadily increasing. The track of this increase in CO_2 levels is called the **Keeling curve.**

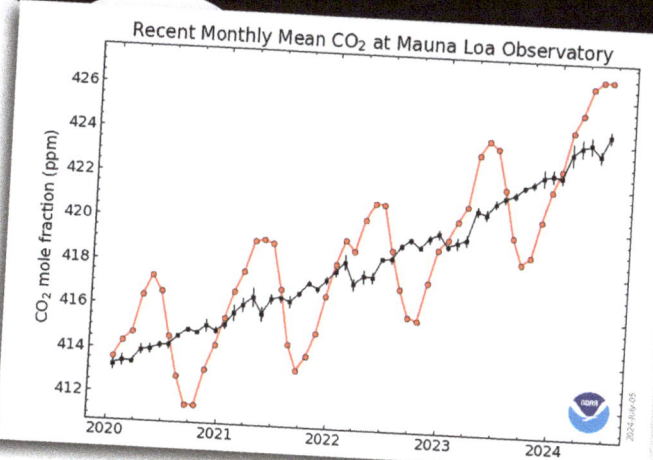

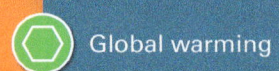 Global warming

Greenhouse effect

Earth is bathed in sunlight. But, the planet doesn't absorb all the heat that lands on it. About 30% of the sun's incoming energy bounces right off the *atmosphere.* The atmosphere absorbs another 30%. The remaining 40% reaches Earth's surface. The warmed surface then sends most of the heat back into the atmosphere.

Here's where things get interesting. Greenhouse gases in the atmosphere absorb the heat emitted by Earth's surface. Each *molecule* then re-radiates that heat in all directions. About half of the heat gets radiated up toward space, and half comes back down toward the ground.

Solar radiation is reflected by Earth's atmosphere.

Infrared radiation is emitted by Earth's surface.

Some solar radiation passes through the atmosphere and warms Earth.

Greenhouse gases absorb infrared radiation.

There's a blanket covering Earth? In a way, yes! Carbon dioxide and other gases trap heat in a manner called the *greenhouse effect*.

The greenhouse effect is necessary for life on Earth. Without the greenhouse effect, the average temperature of Earth's surface would be about 59 Fahrenheit degrees (33 Celsius degrees) colder. Imagine if an average winter day was that much colder. Brr!

You can have too much of a good thing. Increasing levels of carbon dioxide are intensifying the greenhouse effect. More of the sun's heat is being trapped in the atmosphere. The added heat is changing climates and creating more unpredictable and extreme weather patterns.

CURIOUS CONNECTIONS

PLANETOLOGY

Scientists don't have to peer into the future to study the greenhouse effect. The planet closest to us, Venus, swelters under a runaway greenhouse effect. It's over 850 °F (450 °C) at the surface! Venus was cooler in the past—and might have had oceans of water. Why did Earth stay cool while Venus spiraled into heat? That's a question for *comparative planetology*. Studying the similarities and differences between heavenly bodies can help us learn more about Earth and other planets!

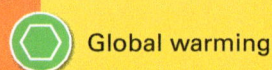

Global warming

Other greenhouse gases

Methane is a potent greenhouse gas. It is more than 28 times more powerful than carbon dioxide in terms of trapping heat. Much of the methane released by humans comes from the beef and dairy industries—from the burps of cattle!

Excuse me!

Nitrous oxide is a greenhouse gas produced by agriculture. When too much fertilizer is applied to farm fields, bacteria absorb the excess and release nitrous oxide as a byproduct. Similarly, the storage and treatment of animal wastes feed bacteria that produce nitrous oxide.

Carbon dioxide isn't the only greenhouse gas. Other *molecules* join it in warming the planet.

Water vapor is yet another greenhouse gas. It cycles through the *atmosphere* in large amounts—think clouds and rain—so human activities don't add to it significantly. Water vapor is still important in global warming, however, because it acts like a warming amplifier. Warmer temperatures cause more water to evaporate, trapping even more of the sun's heat. Kind of like the screechy feedback when a microphone comes too close to a speaker. Ouch!

In the lower *atmosphere* *ozone* **is a greenhouse gas.** It's also a harmful pollutant!

Testing, one-two...

CAREER CORNER

Want to study how the climate has changed over millions of years or predict how it will change in the future? Become a *climatologist!* Climatologists in the field collect data from ice cores, fossils, tree rings, and weather balloons. These data are used to create simulations of past and future climate conditions.

AIR POLLUTION

Excess carbon dioxide and other greenhouse gases in the *atmosphere* are affecting the planet on a global scale. But, they aren't directly harmful to living things. Right at this moment, you're breathing in a few dozen more CO_2 parts per million than your grandparents did, and you're no worse for the wear. Other kinds of emissions, however, can directly harm people and other living things. Such emissions are called *air pollution*. Overall, air pollution contributes to millions of deaths worldwide each year, according to the World Health Organization.

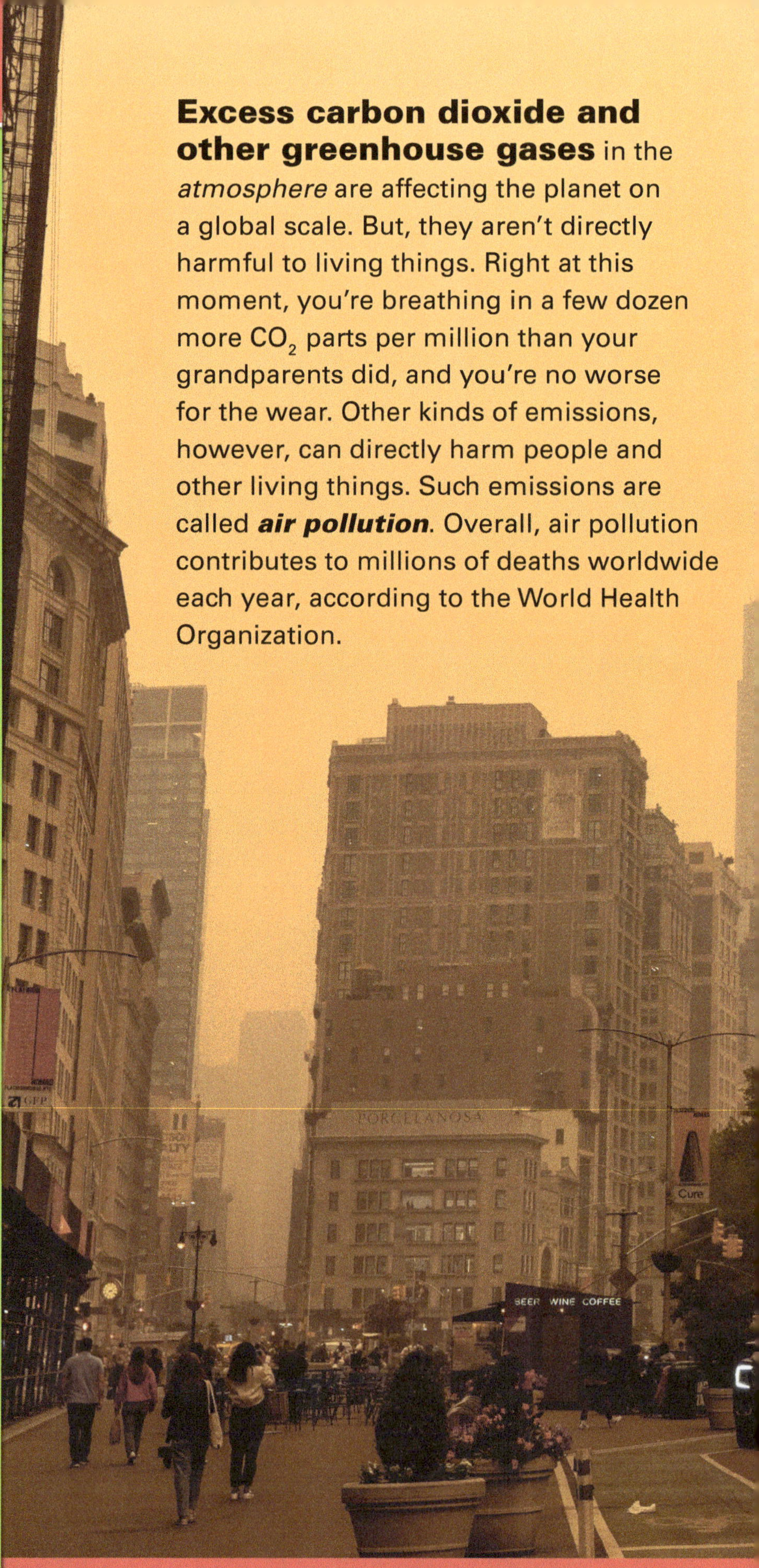

Dirty air is a big problem. Pollution in the air can sicken people, degrade natural habitats, and even damage buildings!

Air pollution isn't just a modern problem. People have been suffering from its effects since they started gathering in cities thousands of years ago. The ancient Roman statesman, author, and philosopher **Seneca** wrote of the air pollution in Rome in a letter from the A.D. mid-60's. He said that taking in the fresh country air made him feel like his old self again!

The hazards of city life!

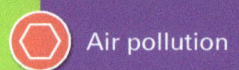
Air pollution

The stench of combustion

Combustion is the main source of air pollution. In a perfect world, carbon-containing fuel would combust completely with oxygen to produce carbon dioxide and water vapor. But sometimes, not enough oxygen reaches the fuel. The result is partial combustion. An extremely poisonous gas called carbon monoxide can form during partial combustion.

$$2C + O_2 \rightarrow 2CO$$

Fuel sources are part of the problem, too. Wood, oil, and coal contain elements other than hydrogen and carbon, such as nitrogen and sulfur. When these elements undergo combustion, they produce nitrogen oxides and sulfur dioxides—serious pollutants. Furthermore, *molecules* of fuel can break apart and disperse into the *atmosphere* without combusting fully.

From tailpipes to smokestacks, lots of air pollutants are byproducts of combustion.

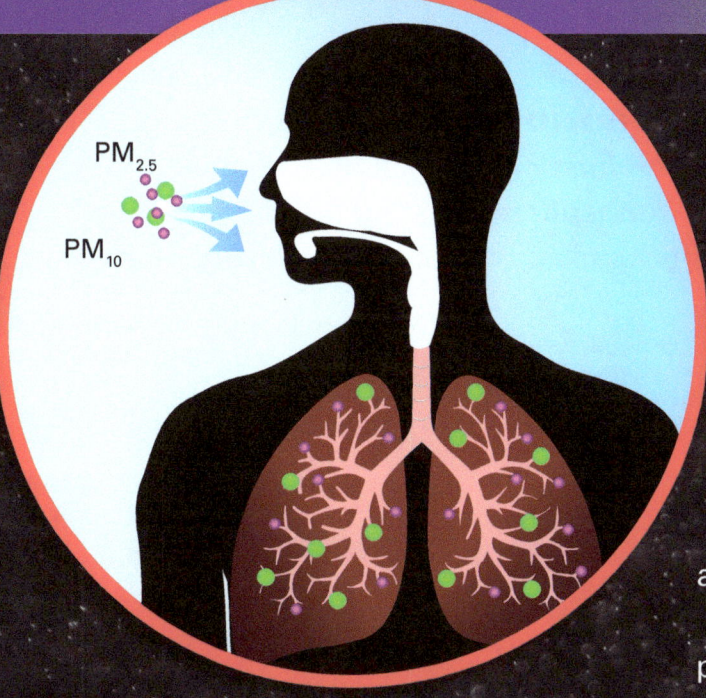

The air pollutants from combustion aren't just gaseous. Tiny solid pieces of fuel and combustion products can get lofted into the air. These pieces are called *particulates*. Larger particulates have diameters greater than 2.5 microns. A micron is 0.000001 meter, or 1/25,400 inch. Small particulates have diameters of 2.5 microns or less. Such small particles are known as fine particles or $PM_{2.5}$. Their tiny size contributes to their harmfulness. Larger particulates get lodged in the lungs. $PM_{2.5}$ can enter the bloodstream. Yikes!

TECH TIME

Can you just live in a dome to get away from air pollution? Sort of! Some buildings, parks, and sports fields in areas with high pollution are covered with domes. Air is filtered and pumped into the dome, inflating it like a balloon. Of course, this is an expensive and yet only partial solution to the pollution problem.

Air pollution

Smog out

Remember those photochemical reactions? They're back! Smog develops when certain gases released by the *combustion* of gasoline and other petroleum products react with sunlight in the *atmosphere*, creating hundreds of harmful chemicals. It's sometimes called photochemical smog for this reason.

Smog can irritate the eyes, nose, and throat and worsen such respiratory ailments as asthma and bronchitis. It can make a person more susceptible to respiratory infections. *Particulates* in smog remain in the lungs and body long after exposure and cause all kinds of health problems. Long term exposure to some of the pollutants in smog can cause cancer and birth defects.

The word **"smog"** was first used in 1905 to describe the combination of smoke and thick fog that sometimes hung over cities in the United Kingdom.

All the different individual air pollutants from combustion mix in the atmosphere to form a toxic cocktail: smog. Smog can cause a variety of health problems.

Sometimes smog can be impossible to get away from! Such weather conditions as a lack of wind or a thermal inversion— in which a layer of warm air settles over cool air near the ground—can cause smog to build up in an area and prevent it from dispersing.

To add insult to injury, smog makes it just plain hard to see!

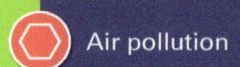 Air pollution

Other sources of air pollution

Volatile organic compounds (VOC's) are carbon-containing *molecules* that can vaporize at standard pressure and everyday temperatures. VOC's are found in all kinds of products, from chemical sprays to couches. Outdoors, such molecules can form smog through photochemical reactions. Indoors, VOC's can be a health hazard.

I'm a boon to comfort but a bane to indoor air quality!

Combustion **isn't the only source of air pollution.** Exotic molecules from industrial processes and chemical sprays vaporize and drift into the *atmosphere*.

Some air pollution is natural. Wind regularly sweeps up dust, pollen, soil particles, and some gases. Volcanic eruptions can pollute the air. Forest fires are a natural source of combustion pollutants. However, global warming is making forest fires more frequent and intense, so how natural some are now is in doubt. And, "natural" doesn't mean "good." Natural pollutants present real health problems to people, both by themselves and in conjunction with human-caused pollution.

DID YOU KNOW?

Many air pollution types run together. For example, products of incomplete fuel burning during *combustion* are also VOC's.

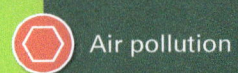
Air pollution

Air pollution and the environment

***Air pollution* can harm plants.** It can slow their growth and make them more susceptible to pests and diseases. Over time, these effects can change the makeup of an ecosystem's plants. Species (kinds) more resistant to pollution will eventually take over. These plants might not be native to the environment, or they might not be what local animals need to thrive. Whatever the case, the ecosystem may permanently change.

Sulfur dioxides and nitrogen oxides can cause damage in a special way. They react with water vapor in the air, forming acids. This is called acid rain when it falls to Earth. But it can take other forms, such as snow or sleet. Acid rain can harm the environment in various ways. It can kill fish and other wildlife in lakes, rivers, and streams. Scientists also think high concentrations of acid rain can harm forests and soils. Acid rain can even damage buildings, bridges, and statues. Yikes!

The whole world is connected through the environment. Air pollution doesn't just harm people, and it doesn't just stay in the air.

Acid rain isn't the only way air pollution can harm the built environment. Smog can also cause building materials to deteriorate faster.

As acid rain shows, what's in the *atmosphere* doesn't necessarily stay there. Some air pollutants fall out of the atmosphere and end up in the water or soil, where they cause additional problems.

5

CLEANING UP THE AIR

Around the world, communities are doing what they can to fight *air pollution* and global warming. Government leaders are pledging difficult cuts to greenhouse gas emissions. Scientists and engineers are improving clean power generation and devising cleaner manufacturing methods. But most of the time, regular people take the lead in the fight against climate change and pollution, for example by easing up on car travel or eating less meat.

We can't allow our air to be choked by pollution and our planet to be baked by climate change. People around the world are taking action.

DID YOU KNOW?

Greta Thunberg began her career as a climate activist at the age of 15! She camped outside the Swedish parliament building, demanding action on climate change.

You're never too young to make a difference!

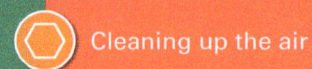 Cleaning up the air

Controlling pollution

Catalytic converters are devices installed in a vehicle's exhaust system that reduce the harmful pollutants produced by the engine. They use *catalysts* (substances that speed up *chemical reactions*) to convert the three main gaseous pollutants—nitrogen oxides, hydrocarbons, and carbon monoxide—into less harmful substances. The catalyst doesn't get used up in the reaction, so it can host reaction after reaction!

Car Catalytic Converter

Heat shield

Stainless steel catalytic converter body

Exhaust gases
HC (hydrocarbon)
CO (carbon monoxide)
NO (nitrogen oxide)

Catalytic active material
aluminum oxide – Al_2O_3
cerum oxide – CeO_2
rare earth stabilizer
metals – Pt/Pd/Rh

Tail pipe emissions
H_2O (water)
CO_2 (carbon dioxide)
N_2 (nitrogen)

Oxidation catalyst to eliminate CO (carbon monoxide) and unburned hydrocarbons (HC)

Reduction catalyst to eliminate NO (nitrogen oxide)

Major reaction
$2CO + O_2 = 2CO_2$
$H_4C_2 + 3O_2 = 2CO_2 + 2H_2O$
$CO + NO = CO_2 + N_2$

Remember that partial *combustion* can create pollutants. What if you just combust those air pollutants? Regenerative thermal oxidizers (RTO's) are special devices added to certain factories. They mix exhaust gas with oxygen and hold them together in a high-temperature chamber. This causes most of the pollutants to combust, producing heat to continue the process.

How do we care for the air?

One way is by destroying pollutants before they reach the *atmosphere*.

Catalytic converters, RTO's, and other pollution mitigation devices cost money. But treating people sickened by air costs far more. Efforts to curb *air pollution* more than pay for themselves in terms of improved human health. Clearing the air is also the right thing to do!

CAREER CORNER

Who designs catalytic converters, RTO's, and other devices that clean the air? Engineers! Engineering is the profession that puts scientific knowledge to practical use. It's applied science!

 Cleaning up the air

Fighting global warming

We put the excess carbon dioxide into the air, and we can take it out. Direct air capture (DAC) is the removal of carbon dioxide directly from the *atmosphere*. The CO_2 gathered by DAC is pure, so it can be used for other purposes. Today, DAC companies are providing extra CO_2 to greenhouses, where it helps plants grow. Soon, it might be used in making soft drinks and sparkling water. Refreshing!

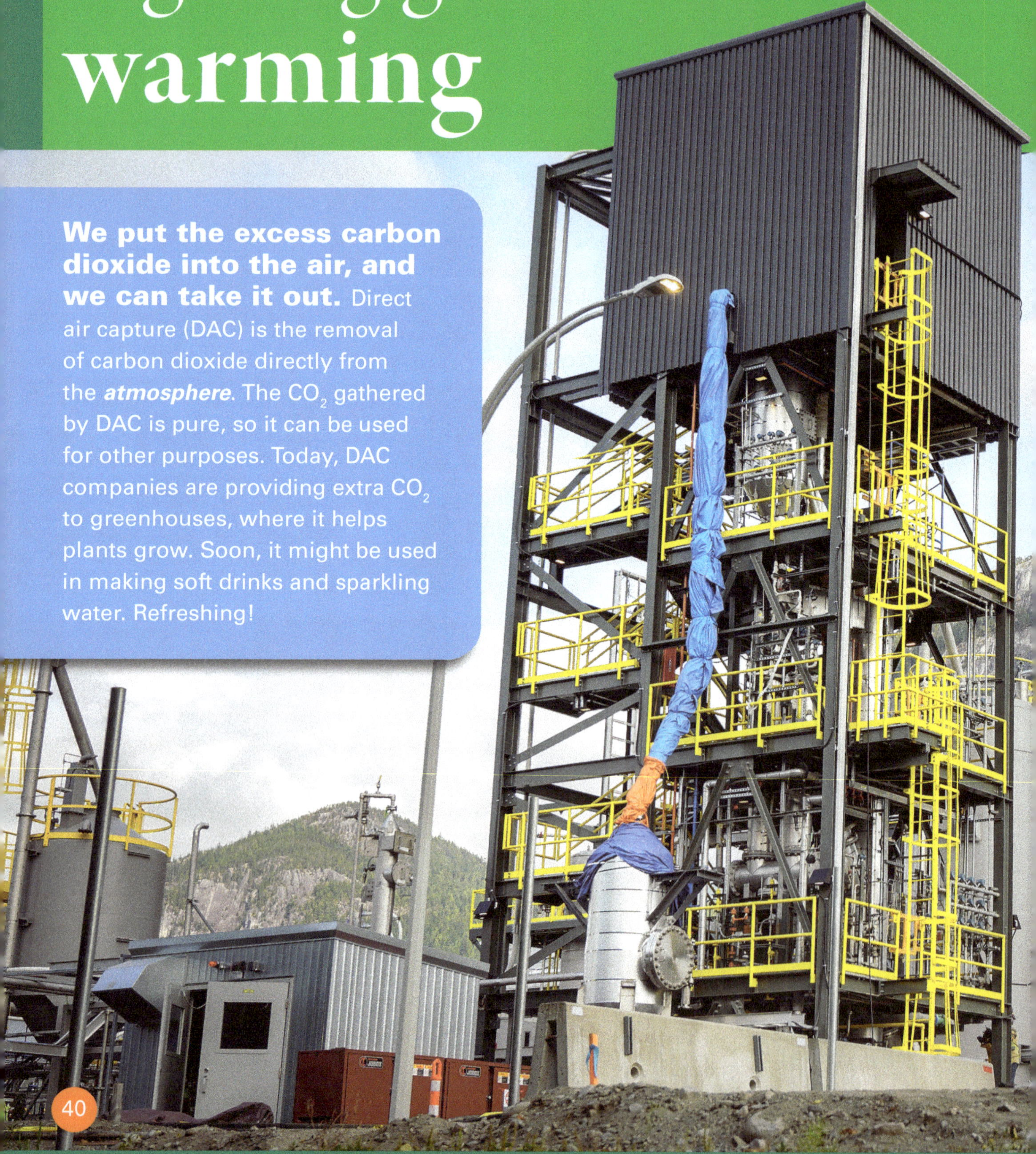

Curbing global warming is the biggest challenge humanity faces today. But, we can do it! Big technological advancements are on the horizon that will slow the rise of global temperatures—if humanity commits to them.

TECH TIME

Rock near Earth's surface undergoes weathering. The action of wind, water, and air breaks down the rock and turns it into different kinds of rock. Some kinds of rocks absorb CO_2 as they weather! But, they're not always at Earth's surface, and such absorption through natural weathering can take a long time. What if we could speed up the process and put weathering to work for us? Enhanced weathering involves grinding up such rock and spreading it out to absorb carbon dioxide. One company, called Silicate, uses discarded concrete as its feedstock. Silicate is partnering with farmers to scatter the ground-up concrete over their fields.

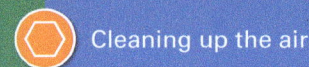 Cleaning up the air

What can YOU do?

International emissions agreements? Great! High-tech *atmosphere* scrubbers? Awesome! But, unless you're a government official, engineer, or big-money philanthropist, there's not a lot you can do to move those things along. There's plenty you *can* do, however, to help clean up the air.

Eat less meat and animal products. Pound-for-pound, plant-based foods are responsible for far fewer greenhouse gas emissions than meat. You don't have to go completely vegetarian or vegan if you don't want to. Try meatless Mondays or only eating meat for dinner. Every little bit helps!

Don't wait for someone else to take care of the air. You can help!

Take a walk! Passenger road travel accounts for 10 percent of greenhouse gas emissions worldwide. Walk or ride a bike to closer destinations. It's great exercise, too!

Limit fires. Cozying up around a warm fire feels nice, but it's not great for the environment. Try to reserve wood-burning fires for special occasions. Don't burn leaves! If your region doesn't collect them, chop them up with your lawn mower and leave them on the grass. Or, use them as the base of a compost pile.

TECH TIME

Lots of yard equipment and motor scooters use two-stroke engines. Such engines are simpler to build and maintain than the four-stroke designs that power many automobiles. But, two-stroke engines produce even more *air pollution* per watt of power they generate. The good news is that high-capacity rechargeable batteries are here! Purchase a battery-powered lawnmower if you can. If you're a kid, volunteer to cut your lawn for a year if your parents get one!

Experimenting with air

What you'll need:
Weigh a balloon
- Balloon
- Food scale or balance

What you'll need:
Snuff out a candle
- Two very small candles
- Two heat-resistant plates
- One tall glass
- Match or lighter

Give it a try

It's easy to forget, but the air around you has weight! Don't believe it? Try this experiment to see for yourself.

1. Weigh an empty balloon on a food scale.
2. Now, blow it up as much as you can (before it pops!) and tie it.
3. Weigh the full balloon.
4. Did the weight go up?

Give it a try

Combustion needs oxygen, and it depletes it pretty quickly from the air.

1. Place candles on separate plates.
2. Have an adult light them one right after the other. (Never experiment with fire without supervision!)
3. Have the adult carefully lower the glass over one of the candles.

Eventually, this candle will dim and flicker out, while the other candle keeps burning.

Air can be hard to study because it's invisible and it's everywhere! Here are some experiments like those that early scientists used to learn more about the properties of air. Give them a try!

Try this next!

Get a helium-filled balloon and weigh it! Then pop it and weigh the pieces. Did it weigh more or less when it was filled with helium?

QUESTION TIME!

What do you think would happen if you quickly moved the glass over to the other candle? Do you think it would stay lit for longer, shorter, or the same time as the first candle? Why do you think so?

45

Index

A
acid rain, 34-35
argon, 13
atoms, 5, 7-8, 10, 14

B
bacteria, 14, 24
Black, Joseph, 20
bonds between atoms, 14-15

C
carbon, 14, 17, 21, 28, 32
carbon dioxide, 13-14, 17, 20-21, 23-26, 28, 38, 40-41

carbon monoxide, 28, 38
catalysts, 38
catalytic converters, 38-39
chemical reactions, 5, 8-9, 12, 16, 38
   see also photochemical reactions
chlorofluorocarbons (CFC's), 11
climate change, 23, 25, 36-37
   see also global warming
climatology, 25
combustion, 16-17, 21, 28-31, 33, 38, 44
comparative planetology, 23

D
direct air capture (DAC), 40
dry ice, 20

E
electrons, 8, 14
engineering, 39
extinction, 19

G
global warming, 18-25, 33, 36, 40-41
   stopping, 40-43
greenhouse effect, 22-23
greenhouse gases, 22-26, 36, 42-43
guano, 15

H
Haber, Fritz, 15
helium, 45
hydrocarbons, 38
hydrogen, 9, 14
hydroxyl radicals, 8

I
infrared rays, 22

K
Keeling, Charles, 21
Keeling curve, 21

L
Lavoisier, Antoine, 17
lightning, 9

M
Mars, 7
methane, 8, 24
molecules, 5, 7-12, 14, 20, 22, 25, 28, 32-33

N
nitrogen, 9, 12-15, 21, 28, 38
nitrogen oxides, 9, 28, 34, 38
nitrous oxide, 24

O
oxygen, 9-10, 12-14, 16-17, 21, 28, 38, 44
ozone, 8, 10-11, 25

P
particulates, 29-30
photochemical reactions, 8, 10, 30, 32
photochemical smog, 30
photochemistry, 8
photons, 8
photosynthesis, 6, 20
pollution, 26-36, 38-39, 43
    controlling, 36-39, 42-43

R
radicals, 8
regenerative thermal oxidizers (RTO's), 38-39
respiration, 6, 30
Rutherford, Daniel, 14

S
Seneca, 27
smog, 30-32, 35
sublimation, 20
sulfur, 28
sulfur dioxides, 28, 34
sun, 6, 8, 10-11, 20, 22-23, 25, 30

T
Thunberg, Greta, 37
Titan, 7

U
ultraviolet rays, 8, 10-11

V
Venus, 23
volatile organic compounds (VOC's), 32-33
volcanic eruptions, 33

W
water vapor, 13, 17, 21, 25, 28, 34
weathering, 41

Glossary

air pollution (air puh LOO shuhn)—the contamination of the air, particularly by industrial waste gases, fuel exhaust, or smoke

atmosphere (AT muh sfihr)—the mass of gases that surrounds a planet or moon

catalyst (KAT uh lihst)—a substance that speeds up chemical reactions

chemical reaction (KEHM uh kuhl ree AK shuhn)—a process by which one or more substances are converted into one or more different substances

climatologist (KLY muh TOL uh jihst)—a scientist who studies climate and climatic conditions

combustion (kuhm BUHS chuhn)—a chemical reaction that gives off heat and light. Combustion involves the rapid combination of oxygen with a fuel to produce burning

greenhouse effect (GREEN HOWS uh FEHKT)—a process that traps heat in Earth's or some other planet's atmosphere, causing the surface temperature to rise

molecule (MOL uh kyool)—the smallest particle into which a substance can be divided and still have the chemical identity of the original substance

particulates (pahr TIHK yuh lihts)—extremely tiny bits of material suspended in the air. Particulates form a major hazard of air pollution.

photochemistry (foh toh KEHM uh stree)—the branch of chemistry that deals with the chemical reactions that result when the molecules of a substance absorb light

photon (FOH ton)—a particle of light

radical (RAD uh kuhl)—a group of two or more charged or neutral atoms that have at least one unpaired electron

www.ingramcontent.com/pod-product-compliance
Lightning Source LLC
Chambersburg PA
CBHW061250170426
43191CB00041B/2406